People Who Went To Hell

DAG HEWARD-MILLS

Parchment House

PEOPLE WHO WENT TO HELL

Copyright © 2023 Dag Heward-Mills

First published by Parchment House 2023

Published by Parchment House 2023
1st Printing 2023

Find out more about Dag Heward-Mills
Healing Jesus Campaign
Write to: evangelist@daghewardmills.org
Website: www.daghewardmills.org
Facebook: Dag Heward-Mills
Twitter: @EvangelistDag

ISBN: 978-1-64330-513-4

Contents

CHAPTER 1

Where Did They Go?

Your fathers, where are they? And the prophets, do they live for ever?

Zechariah 1:5

Where did all the people who died go?

All over the world, funerals are held everyday. You probably attended one not long ago!

One sight that is common in every city, every town, and every village, is a funeral procession or burial service.

In Ghana, cemeteries get very busy at weekends. And though we would rather not think about it, funerals are a constant reminder that in the midst of life, death is ever present with us.

During memorial services, glowing tributes are paid to the dead even if they were bad people! We sob and show our grief with mournful church music in the background.

I have had the opportunity of observing how funerals are conducted in different places.

In one funeral, the house in which the funeral was conducted was renovated and painted nicely. A new road leading to the funeral grounds was constructed.

The dead body had different changes of clothing throughout the evening.

In another funeral, the dead person was dressed in six different types of Kente cloth (an expensive hand woven traditional cloth from Ghana). His Kente cloth was changed six times during the night.

At yet another funeral, the dead body was dressed up in Kente cloth and then it was changed into a suit. Then later on he was dressed up as a Freemason.

At another funeral, a special bed on which the dead body was to be laid in state was imported from another country.

At yet another funeral, people filed by the dead person and everyone kissed the corpse on her lips as part of their farewell.

I am sure that few people think about where the dead person's soul is.

Where do all these departed souls go? Your friends, relations and loved ones who died, "Where did they go?" Think about it. Did they just slip into their graves to "rest in peace"? Or did they vanish mysteriously elsewhere?

What happened to the victims of the First and Second World Wars? What happened to all the slaves who perished when they were carried from Africa to America? What happened to the six million Jews who died in the holocaust? What happened to the one million Tutsis who were killed in Rwanda? What happened to the many people who have died of HIV, Ebola virus and Corona virus? Can anyone tell me where our ancestors are right now?

One thing we know for sure is, they are no longer with us. *So where did they go?*

I remember my horror when, as a new medical student, I first entered the mortuary. The place was filled with the stench of death, and all around me were naked bodies of dead men, women and children. Some were young, others were old. Many had been struck down in the prime of life. Rich and poor lay there, side by side, all pride and dignity forgotten in that horrible place. Is that the end of mankind?

When a man dies, his spirit leaves his body. Without the spirit the body is dead. When Jesus died on the cross, the Bible makes us to know that He *yielded up* the ghost (Matthew 27:50). This means that He *gave up* the spirit. His spirit came out of His body.

When Stephen was stoned to death, he said, "Lord Jesus, *receive my spirit*." (Acts 7:59).

We can see here that when a man dies, his spirit moves out of the body. The spirit itself does not die. Although the body itself decomposes and returns to dust, the spirit lives on eternally.

I have seen people die on hospital wards. You can almost see their spirits coming out of them as they gasp for their last breath. One minute they are alive, the next minute they are gone!

But where do their spirits go? Let's go beyond the grave and find out where they went. According to God's Word, there is an appointment we must all keep *after* death.

...it is appointed unto men once to die, but after this the judgement:

Hebrews 9:27

Basically, this judgment is a time for separation: when Christ, our Judge, takes those who have yielded their lives to Him, and casts the rebellious sinners into hell.

...and HE SHALL SEPARATE THEM one from another, as a shepherd divideth his sheep from the goats:

Matthew 25:32

Talking about unrepentant sinners, Jesus said:

And these shall go away into everlasting punishment: but the righteous into life eternal.

Matthew 25:46

The fact is, there are only two destinations beyond the grave, HEAVEN and HELL. The spirits of those who were righteous in Christ go to be with the Father in heaven, while the spirits of those who rejected Jesus will be cast down to hell.

Dear friend, there is more to life than marriage, money and your retirement home. I know a man who has a special bank account for his burial. He has everything planned out carefully to the last detail. Others have given elaborate instructions concerning their coffins and their graves. But that is where their plans end. Little do they realize that they are going beyond the grave into heaven or hell.

CHAPTER 2

The Roommate in Hell

There was an Assemblies of God church pastor who had an encounter with the Lord one Sunday evening. He had been invited to speak at a church and his programme ended on a Sunday evening. As soon as he entered his hotel room, the Lord appeared to him and said, "I want you to follow me. I want you to see something."

Apparently, the Lord was not happy with the kind of preaching that was coming from this Assemblies of God pastor.

This pastor had been in university and had quit halfway so that he could serve the Lord. He had actually been a pastor's child and had gone wayward. He repented whilst in university and even left the college at that point and went rather to Bible school.

On the night that the Lord asked him to follow Him, He took him down to the regions of hell. When he got into hell, he saw many people. Most of them were lamenting, screaming, wailing and crying just as the Bible says. The Lord seemed to want to show him the vastness of hell and how many people were in there.

Suddenly, he came across somebody he knew. It was his roommate whilst he was in university. He was shocked beyond measure to find his roommate in hell. "When did you get here?" he asked him.

His roommate said to him, "I came here on Friday. I was involved in an automobile accident and I died on Friday." This pastor could not believe his eyes nor his ears. The Lord would not allow him to speak any further to his roommate and took him away and back up to his hotel room.

Back in his hotel room, this pastor was stunned and wanted to call his mother who also knew his roommate. His mother had visited both of them when they were back in the university and knew his roommate very well. Since it was late Sunday night, he decided to call his mother on Monday morning.

On Monday morning, he called his mother and she blurted out, "Have you heard the news that your roommate was killed in an accident on Friday?" This Assemblies of God pastor was stunned. He realized that he had had a real experience on Sunday night. He had encountered his own roommate in hell. His roommate had gone straight to hell after dying in an accident.

This is how many people die and go straight down into the lowest part of hell. The Lord was trying to get this pastor to take the preaching of pure salvation seriously.

Oh, how many go into hell every day never to return, never to rest and never to be free again. All because there is no one to tell them about Jesus. People go to hell because they do not repent of their sins. God has no pleasure in the death of a sinner (Ezekiel 33:11).

CHAPTER 3

The Businessman in Hell

Who can count the dust of Jacob, and the number of the fourth part of Israel? LET ME DIE THE DEATH OF THE RIGHTEOUS, and let my last end be like his!

Numbers 23:10

There are two ways to die. You can die knowing that you are going straight into the arms of your Saviour. That is how a righteous man dies. A righteous man dies praying to have mercy in the hour of his death.

The other way to die is to die the death of the wicked. The wicked man dies, having rejected God and having rejected His messengers. The wicked man dies having blasphemed and insulted the things of God. He dies in rebellion, surrounded by devils who come to take ownership of another deceived and wicked person.

One day, I met a businessman on a golf course. I spoke to him and said that he had to be born again. He was very angry at my suggestion that he should be born again. He began to shout and to create a scene.

I told him that he should stop shouting and creating a scene, just because I had told him to be born again. "Who do you think you are?" he said. "Do you think you are better than the rest of us? You can't come here and judge us."

I decided to stop speaking because this man was really heated up at my suggestion that he be born again. This fellow golfer actually warned that he could beat me up for what I had said.

In the new year, I met this man again. Yet again, I felt like telling him that he needed to be born again. But because he had threatened to beat me, I decided to just wish him a happy New Year.

A few months later, this man became ill and was admitted at the hospital. His illness became worse and soon he sensed that he may die through the illness.

He then asked his assistant whether he knew how to get in touch with me. His assistant called a few times, trying to reach me.

On one of the occasions, I was at the same place that I had witnessed to him and experienced his vociferous objection to my preaching. I could not believe that this man who had insulted me and threatened me was now asking to see me. The Bible teaches that we should seek the Lord while He may be found. You must accept the Lord while He is available.

Seek ye the Lord while he may be found, call ye upon him while he is near:

Isaiah 55:6

Unfortunately, I was unable to reach this gentleman before he died. But his assistant described his death to me. The Bible says, "Let me die the death of a righteous man." On several occasions, this dying man would point to the foot of the bed and say, "Can you see them?" His assistant would answer, "Can I see who? Who are you talking about?"

The dying man could clearly see something that the assistant could not see. "They are coming for me, I can see them." This man was approaching the gates of eternity and wanted me to pray for him. When the door of salvation was opened to him, he rejected it.

His bed was surrounded by demons! They had come to take him captive and to take him to hell. On several occasions, he screamed and pointed to the demons that surrounded his hospital bed. He finally died a horrible death and I was unable to get to the hospital before he died.

"Let me die the death of a righteous man." What a horrible death it is to know that you are going into damnation and never be able to revert.

CHAPTER 4

The Blind Man in Hell

...Let me die the death of the righteous, and let my last end be like his!

Numbers 23:10

One day, I heard the story of another wicked man who died the death of the wicked. This man had rejected any discussion about God and about Jesus Christ. He did not want to give his life to Christ or pray in any way to God. Instead, this man had given himself to witchcraft, occultism and other wicked practices.

Because he was so steeped in occultic practices, he was very far away from anything Christian. As he got older, he developed diabetes and eventually went blind. When the time came for him to die, he was a blind man.

This man died the death of a wicked man! Even though he was blind, he began to see demons and evil spirits around his bed.

This blind man began to panic on his deathbed, as evil spirits surrounded him in the last days of his life.

He could not revert, he could not change and he could not repent. The last hours of this blind man were spent in fright as he pointed out the evil, wicked spirits that surrounded him, getting ready to seize his spirit as soon as he gave up the ghost.

Imagine that! A man who is totally blind, begins to see just before he dies. And what does he see? Wickedness! Evil spirits! Wicked powers hunting for another soul to take down into the lower parts of hell.

Dear brother, there is a heaven and there is a hell out there. There is a God and we will all have to deal with our Creator one day. There is nothing you or I can do to take away the reality of a permanent hell.

Prisons are a reality on this earth and they will be a reality in eternity. Eternity is not just the end of keeping to time. Eternity is your continued existence outside this realm that we are so accustomed to.

May you spend eternity in the presence of God! May you never find your way into hell!

CHAPTER 5

The Auntie in Hell

Who can count the dust of Jacob, and the number of the fourth part of Israel? LET ME DIE THE DEATH OF THE RIGHTEOUS, and let my last end be like his!

Numbers 23:10

Apastor once told us about an auntie that he had. This auntie had no respect for the church. She would lambast pastors and declare that all ministers of the gospel were bogus. "They are just out for your money," she would say.

"Pastors and prophets are a bunch of thieves. They should go and find a good job and stop deceiving people to give them offerings."

She would say there is no God. There is nothing like a God. It is all in the mind. The pastors are making it up so they can collect money from poor people. There is no God, there is no heaven and there is no hell!

The years passed and she became an old lady. As she lay dying, this young pastor happened to come by the city. He was related to this old lady so they got him to come and see her so he could pray for her.

They told the old lady, "Your nephew who became a preacher is here." This old lady who had not moved for several days suddenly stirred up. She came alive when she heard her nephew's name.

The young pastor was happy to pray for her but she did not want prayer. She stirred in the bed and tried to lift herself up. When she realized that the young pastor was right over her bed, she spoke to him and said,

"Pastor, Pastor, tell me there is no God. Tell me there is no heaven. Tell me there is no hell!"

The young pastor was stunned.

"You want me to tell you that there is no hell? You want me to tell you that there is no heaven and there is no God? But there is a heaven and there is a hell and there is a God."

She insisted that the pastor assure her that hell did not exist; but he could not do that.

The young pastor described how her half-blind eyes were like marbles and her guttural voice faded into her throat as she cried, "Tell me there is no God! Tell me there is no heaven! Tell me there is no hell!"

The young pastor watched his unrepentant and stubborn aunt descend into hell crying, "Tell me there is no God! Tell me there is no heaven! Tell me there is no hell!"

Dear friend, there is a heaven and there is a hell. There is a God and we will all have to deal with our Creator one day. There is nothing you or I can do to take away the reality of a permanent hell. Prisons are a reality on this earth and they will be a reality in eternity. Eternity is not just the end of keeping to time. Eternity is your continued existence outside this realm that we are so accustomed to.

May you spend eternity in the presence of God! May you not ever be found in hell!

CHAPTER 6

The Rich Man in Hell

The SORROWS OF HELL compassed me about; the snares of death prevented me;

2 Samuel 22:6

Hell is a place of sorrows, pain and torment! There are only two destinations beyond the grave: heaven or hell. Hell is not a reform school. Hell is a permanent destination.

...I go and prepare a place for you...that where I am, there ye may be also.

John 14:3

Jesus warns us about hell and its unimaginable horrors, and offers us a wonderful and better alternative called heaven.

One reason why we believe in the existence of hell is that Jesus Himself preached more about hell than many other subjects!

For example, in the sixteenth chapter of Luke, Jesus recounts the story of the rich man and Lazarus in graphic detail. Notice that this is no parable.

Jesus has lived in eternity with the Father for millions of years. Perhaps, Jesus particularly remembers when this rich man died and went to hell. Perhaps, that is why He told the story in such graphic detail. Jesus told us how the rich man went to hell.

There was a certain rich man, which was clothed in purple and fine linen, and fared sumptuously every day: And there was a certain beggar named Lazarus, which was laid at his gate, full of sores, And desiring to be fed with the crumbs which fell from the rich man's table: moreover the dogs came and licked his sores. And it came to pass, that the beggar died, and was carried by the angels into Abraham's bosom: the rich man also died, and was buried;

Luke 16:19-22

Rich men are likely to live longer than the poor because they can afford better health care. However, both the rich and the poor will eventually die. Death is the leveller that will level out things for both the rich and the poor.

Even though the rich man's body was put into a grave, the rich man himself was alive in hell. All dead people are still alive! All this was happening in a particular place called a "place of torment". These terrible events actually occurred somewhere. And that place is hell.

And in hell he lift up his eyes, being in torments...

Luke 16:23

The rich man went to hell and Lazarus went to heaven. You will not just stop existing! You are not just converted into a piece of meat! You will head for a permanent destination away from this earth – heaven or hell.

And in hell he lift up his eyes, being in torments, and seeth Abraham afar off, and Lazarus in his bosom. And he cried and said, Father Abraham, have mercy on me, and send Lazarus, that he may dip the tip of his finger in water, and cool my tongue; for I AM TORMENTED IN THIS FLAME.

Luke 16:23-24

When Jesus told the story of Lazarus, he referred to different body parts such as the tongue, the finger and the eyes. It is evident that there is another man within you. This inward man will live forever in heaven or in hell. Note that though his body had been buried, he could still *see, hear* and *feel* tormented.

Hell from beneath is moved for thee to meet thee at thy coming: it stirreth up the dead for thee, even all the chief ones of the earth;...

Isaiah 14:9

The rich man's arrival in hell did not go unnoticed. Hell will be moved to meet you at your coming. The rich man had to lift up his eyes to see Abraham afar off. The rich man was down below and Lazarus was up above him.

The endless nature of the agonies of hell is depicted by the worm that does not die and the fire that is not quenched. "And if thy hand offend thee, cut it off: it is better for thee to enter into life maimed, than having two hands to go into hell, into the fire that never shall be quenched: Where their worm dieth not, and the fire is not quenched" (Mark 9:43-44).

And he cried and said, Father Abraham, have mercy on me, and send Lazarus, that he may dip THE TIP OF HIS FINGER IN WATER, and cool my tongue; for I am tormented in this flame.

Luke 16:24

Nobody asks for a bottle of water in hell! No one asks whether the water is cold or not! No one asks for ice! No one even asks for a small glass of water! Just a drop of water would make all the difference in hell.

Then he said, I pray thee therefore, father, that thou wouldest SEND HIM to my father's house:

Luke 16:27

Clearly, the rich man was used to sending people on errands. In hell, he was no longer able to do that. In the story that Jesus told, the rich man tried to send the poor man Lazarus on an errand, but he was blocked. Things had changed and the rich man was no longer allowed to have his own way.

But Abraham said, Son, REMEMBER THAT THOU IN THY LIFETIME RECEIVEDST THY GOOD THINGS, and likewise Lazarus evil things: but now he is comforted, and thou art tormented.

Luke 16:25

In hell, the rich man remembered the opportunities he had! In hell, you will remember the messages you heard! You will remember your sins, and you will remember the altar calls you did not respond to. You will appreciate the value of gospel crusades, evangelistic breakfast meetings, gospel concerts,

Christian literature and tracts, and Christian television outreach programs. You will wish there had been more of these highly criticized preachers. You will wish you could swallow any words of criticism you have ever uttered against pastors and evangelists.

You will wish you had lived your life with the reality of heaven and hell always on your heart.

CHAPTER 7

Billy and Freddy in Hell

Billy and Freddy Reagan, 1957

The brothers, Billy and Freddy, went to hell. This is the amazing story of how someone saw Billy and Freddy in hell and survived to tell us.

[2] *"One day I decided to take my little son, Ronnie Paul, to a town called Pigeon Ford, and a little market there. As I started to go through the entrance door to the market, another man was coming out. He wouldn't back off and neither would I. The hatred and violence just rose up in me and I busted his head right in the doorway. He fell into a stacked up case of bottles and they burst and went all over the store.*

People were screaming and running, but he picked up a broken bottle and came swinging for my face. As I lifted my left arm to try and stop the blow, he severed all the ligaments, tendons and the artery in my arm. In a fit of rage, I hit him again and kicked at him but this time with that bottle, he severed the Achilles tendon and the arteries in my leg. In minutes the blood was pumping out of my body like out of a water hole.

Every time my heart beat the blood would squirt out and I quickly became faint. The man who ran the market told me that unless I got to the hospital quickly I would be dead. So he got me into the passenger side of my car while he drove, whilst my young son, watching it all, was screaming - completely hysterical. By the time we reached the hospital the floor well of the passenger side was awash with my blood - my feet were wallowing in it. I could hear voices but couldn't open my eyes anymore, because all my strength had gone. When they rolled me into the emergency room I could hear the doctors and nurses saying, 'He's going to need extensive surgery. Transfer him to the hospital in Knoxville.' They loaded me into the ambulance and got me ready for transfer to Knoxville.

Someone had got hold of Elaine and she rushed to the hospital and got into the ambulance with me, as we set off. A young man, about 21 or 22, the paramedic, looked in my face and said, 'Sir, do you know Jesus Christ?' I cursed him and God, with all the strength left in my body. 'There is no God. Who is this Jesus you are talking about? Look at me. Do you think there is a God?' The young man just looked at me and said, 'He loves you, Jesus will help you. Call on Him.' Something inside of me caused me to foam and spit and cry out, 'God, if You really exist, help me. I can't help myself. Help me please.' The young man continued saying, 'Jesus died for you, He gave His life for you.' And all the time I listened, I could hear my wife sobbing.

Smoke filled the ambulance. I couldn't breath, I couldn't see. I thought the ambulance was on fire! What's wrong?' I called out, 'I can't see.' Then through the smoke I started hearing different voices, 'Razor. Razor Reagan. Ronnie! Turn around, don't come here. Go back, stop now. Don't come here!' As I kept hearing these voices, the smoke opened up and I could see what looked like the old quarry pit that we used to swim in when I was a child. In fact it looked exactly like it did on the night we poured gasoline into it and set the water on fire. It was burning and blazing and I was getting nearer to that pit. I could see people in there, and they were burning. Their arms, their faces, their bodies were blazing and the fire wasn't going out. And they were screaming my name!

Closer and closer I went until I could see the individuals, but I couldn't understand what I was seeing. THERE WERE TWO STANDING CLOSE TOGETHER AND I SAW THEY WERE BILLY AND FREDDY, MY TWO BROTHERS, AND THEY WERE BURNING AND SCREAMING. 'What are you doing here?' I yelled, 'You died on the highway in a 1957 Chevrolet, drunk, when you hit the block wall doing 100mph. What are you doing here?' They said, 'Don't come here, there's no way out, It's horrible. Don't come here!!'

I looked to the side. 'Oh, no. Charles! Charles, what are you doing here? Last time I saw you, you were in Pigeon River. We couldn't get the car off you because we were all drunk. When you went into the river we couldn't get you out! We saw your face looking up through the water but we couldn't get you out!'

'Go back', he said, 'Don't come here.'

I looked and could see flower children standing against the wall just like I'd seen them in the sixties, dazed. Flower children so blown away. The age of Aquarius! And I saw many that had overdosed and died. Then I saw my friend, Richard. 'Oh Richard, I can't help you. When we robbed the liquor store in Atlanta, you didn't know what you were doing. You had an old pistol that didn't have any bullets in it and you didn't even ask for the money. But the man didn't know your gun wasn't loaded and he reached under the counter and pulled out a 357, fired point blank and blew your heart out of your chest. You fell against a parking meter and slipped down in the broken glass with the wine and the blood spilling over you. The last thing you said was, 'Oh God.' Richard cried out, 'Don't come here. You can't help.'

I cannot convey the horror, the terror of what I saw and heard. All I knew was I didn't understand it. Suddenly everything went black and I woke up.

Forty-eight hours later I came round in the hospital. My wife was sitting beside me. I had hundreds of stitches inside and outside my body. My wife explained that the doctors had decided not to amputate my arm in view of my job as a truck driver. They would keep a close watch on it though. But I wasn't interested in my arm because I remembered what I'd seen. I could not forget!

People now ask me why I cry, run, and dance when I preach. And I think, 'Oh, Jesus, if it happened to them how it happened to me, they'd know why I'm like I am. Oh God, I don't want to hate anybody no more, I don't want to shoot anybody no more. Oh God, I love everybody.'"[2]

CHAPTER 8

The Postman in Hell

Dr. Maurice Rawlings, 1978

The story of Dr. Maurice Rawlings illustrates how after death, you are condemned to hell because you did not believe in Christ.

Dr Maurice Rawlings is a specialist in heart disease. He is the clinical assistant professor of medicine for the University of Tennessee at Chattanooga, a member of the International Committee on Cardiovascular Diseases, a past governor for the American College of Cardiology for the state of Tennessee, founder of the area's regional Emergency Medical Services Council, faculty instructor for the Advanced Cardiac Life Support programmes, and Fellow of the American College of Physicians, the College of Cardiology, and the College of Chest Physicians. He has also been the personal doctor to Pentagon staff, including Dwight Eisenhower. He is the author of several books on near-death experiences and a contributor to many medical journals. He tells this story: [*sic*]

[3] *"Several years ago now, I had to resuscitate a patient who died whilst trying to reproduce by exercise the chest pains he had been suffering - that experience changed both our lives forever.*

The man, a 47-year-old postman, was exercising on the hospital treadmill. We were hoping the exercise would reproduce the chest pains he said he had been getting while exercising at home. But instead of just getting the pain, the electro cardiogram (the machine that shows your heartbeat) went haywire and he dropped dead, his body thrown off the still moving treadmill. I was doing the external heart compressions while the nurses sorted out a drip and breathing bag, and the patient kept saying, 'Doctor, don't stop!'

Whenever I stopped to reach for something, he would scream, 'I'm in Hell again!' Most patients would say, 'Take your big hands off, you're breaking my ribs,' so I knew something was wrong. We had to put a pacemaker down his collarbone vein right there on the floor. He was writhing and blood was spurting everywhere. I was pushing and I told him to shut up and not to bother me with his 'hell business'. I was trying to save his life and he was trying to tell me about some nefarious nightmare he was having whilst in the death throes.

He then asked me something which was the ultimate insult to me as an atheist, which was, 'Doctor, pray for me.' I told him he was out of his mind, I wasn't a minister. Again he asked me to pray for him and the nurses were looking at me with anticipation and a 'you must do it, it's a dying man's wish' look. So I did. I made up a make-believe prayer, a nonsense. I just wanted to get him off my back so I told him to say it after me. I blurted out embarrassed, 'I believe Jesus Christ is the Son of God. Go on say it. Please keep me out of hell. Say it! And if I live, I'm on the hook, I'm yours forever.' I remember that part well because he's been 'on the hook' ever since. Each time we interrupted the heart massage to adjust the pacemaker he'd scream he was back in hell, then he would convulse, turn blue, stop breathing, and his heart would stop beating. But soon after I said the prayer there was no more writhing, no more fighting. He was calm. The next day, still highly sceptical, I asked him to tell me about being in Hell. I told him he had frightened the nurses to death and scared the hell out of me. He said, 'What Hell? After that prayer you said, I remember seeing my mother when she was living, although she had died when I was three years old.' Impossible! He picked her out of a photograph album his aunt brought in next day, but he had never actually seen her. He identified her from her clothing. He had seen her in Heaven. What apparently happened was that he had sublimated the Hell experiences to painless parts of his memory, but after the conversion he had Heaven experiences.

That 'nonsensical' prayer I prayed to humour him not only got the man converted but it got me too. We both became born-again Christians. "[3]

CHAPTER 9

Howard in Hell

Professor Howard Storm, 1985

The story of the art professor Howard Storm illustrates how many people think there is no God but will be surprised when they die:

[4] *"The date was June 1985, and I was in France. I was leading a group of students on an art tour, my wife was with me and it had come to the last day of our trip. In mid-sentence, I fell to the ground, screaming with intense pain in my stomach. An ambulance came and I was rushed to hospital, to be told by the doctor that I had a hole in my duodenum, and I needed an operation. It was a Saturday, I was taken to hospital and given a bed.*

With the pain getting increasingly worse, a nurse came into the room and told me and my wife that they were going to do the operation. At that point I was ready to die. I had hung on, by my fingernails as it were, trying to stay alive, but not anymore.

The problem for me was that I was an atheist. As a teenager, brought up in a liberal Protestant church, I had lost faith and at college became a scientific atheist. Now, facing death, I felt nothing but hopelessness, depression and despair. I felt I was ready to die and I knew that meant I would cease to exist. I told my wife, who was not an atheist, and did have some faith, and she was in tears.

I closed my eyes and became unconscious. I don't know how much time elapsed but I found myself standing next to my body. I opened my eyes and there was a body in my bed. I didn't understand how it was possible to be outside of one's body and yet looking at the body in my bed. Not only that, but I was extremely agitated and upset because I was yelling at my wife to get her attention but she neither saw nor heard me and didn't move at all. I turned to my room-mate but got the same reaction - he too was oblivious to me and I became more and more angry and agitated. It was at that point that I heard voices calling me by name, from outside the room. Initially I was afraid but the voices seemed friendly, and when I went to the doorway of my room I could see figures moving around in a haze; I asked them to come closer, but they wouldn't come close enough for me to see them clearly. I was able to make out only their silhouettes and general feature. These beings kept asking me to come with them and although I asked a lot of specific questions, they evaded them all giving only vague answers, but insisted that I went with them. So I reluctantly agreed.

I continued to ask questions such as where were we going and they told me that I would see when we got there. I then asked who they were and they said they had come to take me. So I followed them and we went on a journey that I know lasted many, many miles. There was no landscape or architecture, just an ever thickening, ever darkening, haze. Even though they refused to tell me where we were going, they implied they would take care of me and had something for me.

Gradually, they became increasingly cruel as it began to get ever darker. The creatures also started making fun of me and some would say to others, 'Hey, be careful, don't scare him off, or, 'Hush it's too soon for that.' What was even worse, they started making vulgar jokes about me. It seemed at first there were about a dozen of these creatures but later on I thought maybe forty or fifty. Still later, it appeared as if there were hundreds or more.

At this point, I said I wasn't going any further. This was a kind of bluff on my part because I didn't know which way was back, or where I was. I couldn't figure out how I could still be in the hospital but have walked as far as I had. The creatures responded by pushing and shoving me and at first I fought back well and was able to hit them in the face and kick them. However, I couldn't inflict any hurt on them and they simply laughed. Then they began with their fingernails and teeth to pick little pieces off me. I experienced real physical pain and this went on for a long time, with me fighting and trying to fend them off. The difficulty was that I was in the centre of a huge crowd, hands and teeth all around me, and the more I screamed and struggled, the better they liked it. The noise was terrible, as was the cruel laughter and constant torment. Then they went further, insulting me and violating me in other ways too horrible to talk about and with conversation which was more gross than could ever be imagined. Eventually I no longer had the strength or ability to fight anymore and I fell to the ground. They appeared to lose interest in me. People seemed to be coming by and giving me a kick but the intense fury had gone.

As I lay there I had the strangest experience. A voice that seemed to come from my chest spoke to my mind. This was an internal conversation and the voice said, 'Pray to God.'

I proceeded to argue with my voice, saying I didn't believe in God so how could I pray to Him. But my voice said, 'Pray to God,' and I thought, 'But I don't know how to pray, I don't know what praying means!' For a third time my voice said, 'Pray to God', so I thought I'd better try. I started to think things like 'The Lord is my Shepherd, God bless America', just little things that I could remember which sounded holy. Soon the thoughts became mutterings and as they did the creatures around me started screaming and yelling at me that there was no God. They told me I was the worst of the worst. Nobody could hear me they said, so what did I think I was doing?

Because these evil creatures were so strong in their protest I started to say more, and shouted things at them like, 'God loves me. Get away from me. In the name of God, leave me alone!' They continued to scream at me except now they were retreating back into the darkness. I finally came to the point where I found myself screaming all the things I could think of that sounded religious but there was nobody around. I was completely alone in the darkness; they had retreated as if my words were pouring scalding water on them.

Although I was shouting little pieces of Psalm 23, 'Yea though I walk through the valley of death, I will fear no evil', and the Lord's Prayer, I didn't believe them. I meant them in the sense that I could see they were having the effect of driving these creatures off, but I wasn't convinced in my heart about the truth of them.

I was there alone. For how long, I don't know, but I sank into great hopelessness, deeper than I could imagine possible. Here I was, in the dark and somewhere out in the darkness were the evil creatures. I couldn't move, I couldn't crawl, I was too torn up and didn't know what to do. In fact I got to the point where I really did not want to exist anymore.

It was at the moment of deepest despair that a tune from my childhood, when I had gone to Sunday school, started going through my head. 'Jesus loves me….Jesus loves me, this I know', and I wanted that to be true more than I have ever wanted anything in my life. With every ounce of my being, my mind, strength and heart, I screamed into the darkness, 'Please Jesus, save me!' I meant it. I didn't question or doubt it, I just meant it with every fibre of my being and upon doing that a small faint star appeared in the darkness. It grew rapidly bright and brighter, and soon it was a large, indescribably brilliant light, which picked me into itself. As it lifted me up I looked down at myself and saw all the rips, tears and wounds that I had received, just slowly disappear.

As I continued to be lifted up, I became whole and well. The only way I can describe it is as something of inexplicable beauty which I knew was good.

One minute I was an atheist, the next minute every part of me wanted Jesus. I lost all of my pride, my egotism, my self-dependence, my reliance on my much-exalted intellect. All of that had ceased to serve me anymore - it had failed me. All the things I had lived my life for and made my god and had worshipped had let me down. What I came to cry out for was a hope that was planted in a small child many years before.

This experience changed my life completely. Not only did I eventually become a full-time minister but it changed the way I felt. Before there used to be melancholy and cynicism, but now there is genuine joy, all the time. That's not to say I don't have my ups and downs, but behind every day there is joyfulness and I try, as best as I can, to spread that joy and peace. "[4]

CHAPTER 10

Ian in Hell

Ian McCormack, 1988

The story of Ian McCormack illustrates how people are surprised when they die:

[5] *"My whole life was centred around sport and travel. At 24 years of age, having taken a veterinary science degree at university in New Zealand, I had just completed two years travelling around the world. Now I was living in an earthly paradise for anyone who loved surfing and scuba diving - Mauritius.*

I used to go surfing and fishing with the local Creole divers and got hooked on night diving. Being used to colder climates than the locals, I only wore a thin 1mm short-sleeved wet suit whereas the locals would wear the full 3-4mm suits and be totally encased from head to foot. Four days before I was due to leave the island and go back to New Zealand for my brother's wedding, I went out night diving with the local boys. I was a bit uneasy about going because I could see an electric storm on the horizon but I let myself be persuaded.

As I dived that night, the beam of my torch light picked out a jellyfish right in front of me. I was fascinated because this one was not the usual shape but 'box-shaped.' Little did I realize as I squeezed it through my leather-gloved hand, that this box jellyfish, or sea wasp, was the second deadliest creature known to man. Its toxin has killed over seventy Australians alone and up in the northern parts of Australia, it had killed more people than had sharks. In Darwin, the sting from this fish stopped the heart of a 38-year-old man in 10 minutes.

Suddenly, I experienced what I felt like a huge electric shock in my forearm, like thousands of volts of electricity. Not being able to see what had happened, I did the worst thing possible, I rubbed my arm, and rubbed in the poison from the tentacles of this fish. Before I could get out onto the reef, I was stung by three other box jellyfish. My forearm was swollen like a balloon and where the tentacles had stung there were burn-like blisters across my arm. I felt on fire as the poison began moving round my body. It hit my lymph gland, as if it had been punched, and my breathing quickly became constricted.

I knew I needed hospitalization and quickly! After I was stung a fifth time, one of the divers rowed me back to shore and dumped me on the road, which was in a desolate part of the island. Lying on my back and feeling the poison taking its effect, I heard a quiet voice saying, 'Son, if you close your eyes you will never wake again.' I had no idea who said it but being a qualified lifeguard and instructor in scuba, I knew unless I got anti-toxin quickly, I would die.

My attempts to get to hospital were fraught to say the least, I had no money and an Indian taxi driver, whom I had begged on my knees for a lift, picked me up but only took me to a hotel and dumped me in the car park thinking he was unlikely to get paid. The Chinese proprietor of the hotel also refused to take me in his car, thinking the marks on my arm were from overdosing on heroin. However, a security guard, who happened to be one of my drinking companions rang for an ambulance.

During the journey, my life flashed before me and I thought, 'I'm going to die. This is what happens before you die, your life comes before you.' Despite being an atheist, I wondered whether there was any life after death. Then my mother's face came before me and said, 'Ian, no matter how far from God you are, if you will only but cry out to God from your heart, God will hear you and God will forgive you.'

I promised God however, that if I came through this experience alive, I would find out what His will for me was and follow Him all the days of my life. As I prayed that prayer I knew I had made peace with God and almost immediately the ambulance doors opened. I was lifted onto a wheelchair and raced into the hospital.

Doctors and nurses rushed in. They attempted to take my blood pressure twice, but they could find no pulse. The doctors gave me injections of anti-toxin and dextrose in an attempt to save my life.

I was conscious of the fact that if I drifted out of my body that would be it - death. I knew this was no weird trip or hallucination, this was real, but I had no intention of leaving my body and dying. I intended to stay awake all night if necessary, and fight the poison in my system.

Feeling myself being lifted onto a recovery bed, I was aware that I could not feel my arms at all and I could no longer keep my eyes open. I couldn't tilt my head, my eyes were filling up with perspiration so that I could hardly see and I remember closing my eyes and breathing a sigh of relief. At that point, from what I can ascertain from the hospital, I was clinically dead for 15 minutes.

The most scary thing for me was that the moment my eyes closed I was suddenly wide awake again, standing by what I thought was my bed, in pitch black darkness, wondering why the doctors had turned out the lights. I decided to switch the lights on and put my hand out to find the wall but I couldn't find a wall. 'OK,' I thought, 'maybe they've moved me to the general ward.' If I could get back to my bed, I could turn the lamp on but I couldn't find my bed. I thought I'd better just stand still for a moment, but it was so dark I couldn't even see my hand in front of my face and if I lifted my right hand up to my face it seemed either to miss it or go straight through.

'You can't miss your head,' I thought to myself, so I put both hands up to my face and they seemed to pass straight through. That was the most weird feeling but what followed was even worse because I realized I could not touch any part of my physical form. Yet I had the sensation of being a complete human being with all my faculties, only I didn't have a fleshly form.

I realize now that I was in fact outside my body because when someone dies, their spirit leaves their body.

My next thought was, 'Where on earth am I?' because I could feel the most intense evil pervading the darkness all around me. It was as if the darkness took on a spiritual dimension. There was a totally evil presence there, which started to move towards me. Although I still couldn't see, I sensed something looking at me out of the darkness. Then to my right came a voice which yelled, 'Shut up!' As I backed off from that voice another one from the left shouted, 'You deserve to be here!' My arms came up to protect myself and I asked, 'Where am I?' and a third voice replied, 'You're in Hell. Now shut up.'

Some people think Hell is just a big party but I tell you it's going to be pretty hard to grab your beer down there and pretty hard to find your face.

I stood there in that blackness long enough to put the fear of God into me for eternity. You might ask why God took me down there, but He told me later that if I hadn't prayed that deathbed prayer in the ambulance, I would have stayed in Hell. Thank God for His grace, which hears a sinner's prayer in the last seconds of his life."[5]

CHAPTER 11

Who Goes to Hell?

The wicked shall be turned into hell, and all the nations that forget God.

Psalm 9:17

S inners go to hell! The wicked will be turned into hell! All the people who forget about God will go to hell!

I have observed, to my amazement, sinfulness in all children. Even if children grow up in a godly atmosphere of love and peace, they are still sinful. Who taught children to be stubborn and disobedient? Who taught them to lie? Where did they pick these traits from? The Bible explains that sin came into the world and into our children through Adam. You see, Adam was the father of the entire human race. And when he sinned, he passed on that sinful nature to all his descendants like a hereditary disease or a family trait.

Wherefore, as by one man sin entered into the world, and death by sin; and SO DEATH PASSED UPON ALL MEN, for that all have sinned:

Romans 5:12

This is why you do not have to teach a child how to lie. He just lies naturally. It comes automatically. Children steal and cheat automatically. They are self-willed and disobedient by nature. It just happens. And you did the same thing when you were a child, because we were all born in sin. We take after our forefather Adam.

For ALL have sinned, and come short of the glory of God;

Romans 3:23

We know from God's Word that the wages of sin is death; everlasting separation from God. Another word for "wages" is payment or salary. Your salary is your entitlement; what you are entitled to, which means what you get for what you have done.

And what we get for being sinners is eternal separation from a righteous God. That is why man in his natural condition is considered *spiritually dead*, instead of being *spiritually alive* to the things of God.

Have you noticed that all over the world the dead are separated from the living? Cemeteries are usually located out of town to separate the living from the dead.

Think about all your loved ones who have died in the past. In spite of all the love you had for them, you could no longer share your home with them because they had developed a condition called "death". They were buried in the graveyard, out of sight. And you left them there, because their condition made it impossible for you to have fellowship with them.

That is exactly how it is with God. A spiritually dead man is separated from a holy God. Unless he is born again spiritually, and reconciled to God through Christ, man is headed for Hell.

Therefore as sin came into the world through one man, and death as the result of sin, SO DEATH SPREAD TO ALL MEN [no one being able to stop it or to escape its power] because ALL MEN SINNED.
Romans 5:12 (AMP)

Adam's sin turned all men into natural sinners. This resulted in a death sentence being passed on all men. This makes us all automatic candidates for hell. In other words, every unsaved soul is bound to end up in hell, from the President to the poorest man in the village.

So you see, it is very easy to arrive at this fearful destination called hell. Even if we just sit down, doing nothing just minding our own business, we will still end up there.

Jesus, in His compassion for mankind urged men to believe on Him so that we would not perish, but have everlasting life.

Unfortunately, most people have not accepted His invitation, and have died in their sins, passing away into hell. Multitudes have literally poured into hell over the years. Multitudes? Do I mean *masses* of people? Yes, I am afraid so!

Enter ye in at the strait gate: for wide is the gate, and broad is the way, that leadeth to destruction, and MANY THERE BE WHICH GO IN THEREAT:

Matthew 7:13

CHAPTER 12

Hell is Below Us

The way of life is above to the wise, that he may depart from hell beneath.

Proverbs 15:24

You might ask, "If there is such a place as hell, then *where* exactly is it?"

Well, according to God's Word, hell is *beneath* us. Its specific geographical location is underground. Down under! Below us!

1. Hell is beneath us.

    HELL FROM BENEATH is moved…to meet thee…

    Isaiah 14:9

2. Hell is a place you are brought down to. Hell is a deep pit you are thrown into.

    Yet thou shalt be BROUGHT DOWN TO HELL, to the sides of the pit.

    Isaiah 14:15

3. Hell is a place you go down into.

    Let death seize upon them, and let them GO DOWN quick into hell: for wickedness is in their dwellings, and among them.

    Psalm 55:15

    And they shall not lie with the mighty that are fallen of the uncircumcised, which are GONE DOWN TO HELL with their weapons of war: and they have laid their swords under their heads, but their iniquities shall be upon their bones, though they were the terror of the mighty in the land of the living.

    Ezekiel 32:27

4. Hell is a place located in the lower parts of the earth. In Ephesians, Paul declared that hell is in the lower parts of the earth. The lower parts of the earth! Just think about it. The lower parts of the earth, that is where hell is!

Wherefore he saith, when he ascended up on high, he led captivity captive, and gave gifts unto men. (Now that he ascended, what is it but that he also descended first into the LOWER PARTS OF THE EARTH?

Ephesians 4:8-9

Those Under the Earth

1. **This scripture speaks of some people or creatures who are under the earth.**

Wherefore God also hath highly exalted him, and given him a name which is above every name: That at the name of Jesus every knee should bow, of things in heaven, and things in earth, and THINGS UNDER THE EARTH;

Philippians 2:9-10

2. **Jesus descended into the lower parts of the earth, where there are many people.**

Wherefore he saith, when he ascended up on high, he led captivity captive, and gave gifts unto men. (Now that he ascended, what is it but that HE ALSO DESCENDED FIRST INTO THE LOWER PARTS OF THE EARTH? He that descended is the same also that ascended up far above all heavens, that he might fill all things.)

Ephesians 4:8-10

3. **There are people under the earth.**

And no man in heaven, nor in earth, NEITHER UNDER THE EARTH, was able to open the book, neither to look thereon.

Revelation 5:3

4. **There are many people under the earth and also under the sea.**

   And every creature which is in heaven, and on the earth, AND UNDER THE EARTH, and such as are in the sea, and all that are in them, heard I saying, Blessing, and honour, and glory, and power, be unto him that sitteth upon the throne, and unto the Lamb for ever and ever.

   Revelation 5:13

5. **Moses warned us not to make images of those creatures under the earth.** Demons inspire men to make grotesque images of themselves.

   Thou shalt not make unto thee any graven image, OR ANY LIKENESS OF ANY THING THAT IS IN HEAVEN ABOVE, OR THAT IS IN THE EARTH BENEATH, OR THAT IS IN THE WATER UNDER THE EARTH:

   Exodus 20:4

6. **Korah and his family are a well known example of those who transitioned in a new way directly into "under the earth".** Never before and never again since then, did a man go directly from living on earth to living under the earth in a second. Usually the body dies and the soul goes there. But this time the body and soul entered together. It shows how God is against those who speak against His anointed.

   But if the Lord make a new thing, and the earth open her mouth, and swallow them up, with all that appertain unto them, and they go down quick into the pit; then ye shall understand that these men have provoked the Lord.

   Numbers 16:30

Someone Went Under the Earth

I remember a very vivid testimony about someone who died and went to hell. He had been stricken with an incurable heart disease which kept him in bed most of the time. The illness got worse till it came to a point where he knew he was dying. Mind you, he had been baptized and had been going to church all his life, *but he was not saved.*

Just after he died, he felt his spirit (his real self, the inner man) coming out of his body. He could see his lifeless body on the bed. THEN HE BEGAN TO GO DOWN. As he went down into the pitch darkness, it became hotter and hotter. When he could go no further, a fearsome, beastly creature emerged from the darkness. The foul, demonic monster grabbed his hand to receive him. Then it began to pull him through the thick darkness towards the unbearable heat.

Suddenly, a voice boomed from above. He did not understand the language. But the hand released him immediately, and his spirit sort of floated back up to the earth and into his body. This happened two more times, and each time his spirit was released to go back to the surface and into his body. I believe this testimony of this man, because it lines up with Scripture. (Luke 16:19-31)

Dear friend, hell is not, a gathering of all departed rock stars for an endless "jam". Mind you, there is no electricity in hell for such concerts. The only thing that is close to singing in hell is *groaning, weeping* and *gnashing* of teeth!

Hell cannot be just a state of mind. Hell actually exists. It is a tangible, physical place and its location is down under in the lower parts of the earth. Even as you read this, some people you know are crying for help that will never ever come.

The souls of men who die without Christ are not just flung into hell indiscriminately. Hell is divided into different areas, prepared for different classifications of people. Hell is characterized by darkness, torment, pain, screaming and horrors.

CHAPTER 13

Hell Has a Reception

Hell from BENEATH is moved...to MEET thee at thy coming...

Isaiah 14:9

There is a reception for all those who arrive down below.

And here, we are not talking about polite receptionists in an air-conditioned office!

When the perished soul arrives in hell, he is met by the most repulsive, foul-smelling, reptilian beasts at the gates of hell. Then he is assigned to the part of hell where the punishment most fits the crime.

For a fire is kindled in mine anger, and SHALL BURN UNTO THE LOWEST HELL, and shall consume the earth with her increase, and set on fire the foundations of the mountains.

Deuteronomy 32:22

Notice the expression here: lowest hell. There are different levels in hell. The lower the level, the greater the torment.

God is a just God. The severity of the punishment will be proportional to the sins committed.

For example, those who have caused the death of so many people through wars, murder and witchcraft, may get a more severe punishment than petty liars.

Even in our earthly legal system there is a sense of fairness in the administration of justice. We pronounce different judgments for different crimes. Even our prisons have different areas and sections within it. That is the way it is in hell. There are higher and lower sectors of hell.

There are various departments reserved for different groups of people.

CHAPTER 14

Hell is Full of "Big Shots"

HELL FROM BENEATH is moved for thee to meet thee at thy coming: it stirreth up the dead for thee, EVEN ALL THE CHIEF ONES OF THE EARTH; it hath raised up from their thrones all the KINGS of the nations.

Isaiah 14:9

Hell will become the permanent address of many CHIEF ONES and KINGS OF THE NATIONS. This refers to kings, emperors, presidents, statesmen, politicians, doctors, lawyers, famous personalities, film stars, millionaires and business tycoons. These are the high and mighty in the society, the wealthy and the influential; the great leaders in history, the chief ones of the earth!

Basically, hell is a "big-shot" society, full of high class and noble people.

This is not to say, of course, that there are no poor people there. The well-known disregard for the things of God by many rich people has over the centuries ended up populating hell. The poor are generally rich in faith. The financially rich are not so rich in faith. That is why not many noble people have chosen the way to salvation.

And why should they? With all the comforts of wealth, the rich and powerful see no need for God. No wonder Jesus said the rich would find it hard to get to heaven. Riches are deceptive. The deceitfulness of riches blinds many people. Rich people are often deceived into thinking that they do not need God.

So where are all the heads of state, pop stars, great philosophers, business magnates and other famous world figures who have died? Did they go to heaven or hell?

And so, whilst we may hold state funerals for them and erect monuments in their honour, the old-timers of hell will be saying to the newcomers: "Art thou also become like us?"

...ART THOU ALSO BECOME WEAK AS WE? art thou become like unto us? THY POMP IS BROUGHT DOWN to the grave, and the noise of thy viols: the worm is spread under thee, and the worms cover thee.

Isaiah 14:10-11

48

Those who are far from God in this life, will be far from God after death. Unfortunately, our glowing tributes will not change their destinations. Neither can their wealth or their achievements buy them a place in heaven.

It should not be surprising then, if hell's roll call will sound like a "Who's Who" of the rich and famous.

CHAPTER 15

Hell is Expanding

Therefore HELL HATH ENLARGED HERSELF, and
OPENED HER MOUTH WITHOUT MEASURE...
                                    Isaiah 5:14

When I became a medical doctor, the authorities began the construction of new blocks of flats, to accommodate the increasing number of newly-qualified doctors. With the inflow of many new doctors, the doctors' apartments had to be expanded. In a similar way, hell is currently undergoing some major rehabilitation and extension works. What for? Hell is expanding in order to cater for the increasing multitudes who are rushing there.

Let us take another look at the Bible's report on the project:

THEREFORE HELL HATH ENLARGED HERSELF, and OPENED HER

MOUTH WITHOUT MEASURE: and their glory, and their multitude, and their pomp, and he that rejoiceth, shall descend into it.

Isaiah 5:14

The mouth of hell is the main gate of hell. This main gate of hell is being worked upon. It is being enlarged!

Hell is being worked on. Hell is being enlarged! That is alarming!

Hell is expecting much more human traffic! Dear friend, preparations are being made to receive you in hell if you do not give your life to Jesus Christ.

The Church of God must sit up. The Church of God must wake up from its slumber.

Christians must rise up and build churches to accommodate souls that are being saved.

There must be construction of churches or there will be construction in hell!

Souls must be accommodated. Souls will either be accommodated in heaven or in hell. May it be the case that we build facilities to host souls on earth and in heaven! May satan be denied new arrivals in the expanded version of hell.

CHAPTER 16

If You Are Not Born Again You Will Go to Hell

Jesus answered and said unto him, Verily, verily, I say unto thee, Except a man be born again, he cannot see the kingdom of God.

John 3:3

U nless you are born again you cannot go to heaven. As a teenager, I regularly attended church and gave offerings, but I never heard anything about being born again. Never! Instead, I was made to understand that if I recited three *Hail Mary's* and *The Lord's Prayer* once a day, I would make it to heaven. However, if I had died, I would have perished in hell, in spite of all my recitations. Ignorance is sending more people to hell than we imagine.

> **THEREFORE MY PEOPLE ARE GONE INTO CAPTIVITY, BECAUSE THEY HAVE NO KNOWLEDGE: and their honourable men are famished, and their multitude dried up with thirst. Therefore hell hath enlarged herself, and opened her mouth without measure...**
>
> **Isaiah 5:13-14a**

Nobody in their right minds would go to hell if they really knew what it was all about. After all, most people want to serve God. That is why they practice religion. Actually, religion is man's *search* for God. But Jesus is the *only* way to God. Anyone who desires to come God can only do so through Jesus.

> **Jesus saith unto him, I am the way, the truth, and the life: no man cometh unto the Father, but by me.**
>
> **John 14:6**

Today, many churches are full of sincere people seeking God. But without the proper teaching from the pulpit about God's plan of salvation, many churchgoers will be disappointed on the last day. Speaking of the Jews, Paul testified that they indeed had a zeal for God, but not according to knowledge.

> **For BEING IGNORANT of the righteousness that God ascribes (which makes one acceptable to Him in word, thought and deed), and seeking to establish**

a righteousness (a means of salvation) of their own, they did not obey or submit themselves to God's righteousness.

Romans 10:3 (AMPC)

What is God's prescription for finding heaven and avoiding hell?

...Except a man be born again, he cannot see the kingdom of God.

John 3:3

My dear friend, YOU MUST BE BORN AGAIN! There is no other option. You must receive Christ as your personal Saviour. Being born again is not a new idea being propagated by some new churches. It is a fundamental, biblical instruction given by Christ to everyone! I know of course, that many people are sincere but mistaken.

I believe that every single Christian, especially pastors, will also give account to God for withholding vital information about the reality of hell. If souls are perishing because of ignorance, then those with knowledge will definitely be held accountable.

CHAPTER 17

Can I be Transferred from Hell?

And beside all this, between us and you there is a great gulf fixed: so that they which would pass from hence to you cannot; NEITHER CAN THEY PASS TO US, THAT WOULD COME FROM THENCE.

Luke 16:26

he rich man found himself in hell. He must have been shocked that he had been put into such a place. The disturbing thing was that he could see Lazarus afar off. "How come I am here and he is there?"

Is it possible to be transferred from hell to heaven? In his desperation, the rich man sent a message to Abraham asking for a possible transfer! But Abraham explained to him that transfer out of hell was not possible! As the anguish of this man worsened, he sent another message asking for a drop of water, not even a glass of water.

Dear friend, make sure you do not get into hell, because once you are there, there is no way out! Hell is a permanent place!

There is a road from earth to heaven. There is another road from earth to hell. But there is no road from hell to heaven! Once you are in, you are stuck.

This is why the message on hell is so important. If you make a mistake about your eternal destiny, you will regret it for eternity.

And shall cast them into the furnace of fire: there shall be wailing and gnashing of teeth.
Matthew 13:50

Hell is a place of weeping and gnashing of teeth. Gnashing of teeth speaks of regret. If you write an important exam and come out of the examination hall only to discover that there was a whole question at the back of the paper which you did not see, you will find yourself gnashing your teeth.

If you find out that it was a question that you could have answered very easily, you will find yourself gnashing your teeth even more. If you find out that it was a compulsory question, you will weep, wail and gnash your teeth.

CHAPTER 18

The Six Different Hells

The wicked shall be turned into hell...

Psalm 9:17a

More Than One Hell

It seems there is more than one hell. There are different places with different names which are also hell. In other words, there are different kinds of hell. Each hell has a different purpose.

Just as there is more than one prison in a country, a number of different names have come up as being the final destination for the dead. Each of these destinations is unique.

Is it possible to be transferred from one hell to another? I do not believe so but as you get to know about the different hells, you will probably know whether you would want to transfer from one to the other. Indeed, there are six different types of hell.

1. HADES

And I say also unto thee, That thou art Peter, and upon this rock I will build my church; and the gates of HELL (*HADES*) shall not prevail against it.

Matthew 16:18

2. PARADISE

And Jesus said unto him, Verily I say unto thee, To day shalt thou be with me in PARADISE.

Luke 23:43

3. BOTTOMLESS PIT

And the fifth angel sounded, and I saw a star fall from heaven unto the earth: and to him was given THE KEY OF THE BOTTOMLESS PIT. And he opened the bottomless pit; and there arose a smoke out of the pit, as the smoke of a great furnace; and the sun and the air were darkened by reason of the smoke of the pit. And THERE CAME OUT OF THE SMOKE LOCUSTS UPON THE EARTH: and unto them was given power, as the scorpions of the earth have power. And it was commanded them that they should not hurt the grass of the earth, neither any green thing, neither any tree; but only those men which have not the seal of God in their foreheads. And to them it was given that they should not kill them, but that they should be tormented five months: and their torment was as the torment of a scorpion, when he striketh a man.

Revelation 9:1-5

4. *TARTARUS*

For if God spared not the angels that sinned, but cast them down to HELL (*TARTARUS*), and delivered them into chains of darkness, to be reserved unto judgment; And spared not the old world, but saved Noah the eighth person, a preacher of righteousness, bringing in the flood upon the world of the ungodly;

2 Peter 2:4-5

5. *GEHENNA*

But I say unto you, that whosoever is angry with his brother without a cause shall be in danger of the judgment: and whosoever shall say to his brother, Raca, shall be in danger of the council: but whosoever shall say, Thou fool, shall be in danger of HELL FIRE (*GEHENNA*).

Matthew 5:22

6. THE LAKE OF FIRE

And the devil that deceived them was cast into the lake of fire and brimstone, where the beast and the false prophet are, and shall be tormented day and night for ever and ever. And I saw a great white throne, and him that sat on it, from whose face the earth and the heaven fled away; and there was found no place for them. And I saw the dead, small and great, stand before God; and the books were opened: and another book was opened, which is the book of life: and the dead were judged out of those things which were written in the books, according to their works. And the sea gave up the dead which were in it; and death and hell delivered up the dead which were in them: and they were judged every man according to their works. AND DEATH AND HELL (*HADES*) WERE CAST INTO THE LAKE OF FIRE. This is the second death. And whosoever was not found written in the book of life was cast into the lake of fire.

Revelation 20:10-15

CHAPTER 19

Hades

And I say also unto thee, That thou art Peter, and upon this rock I will build my church; and the gates of HELL (*HADES*) shall not prevail against it.

Matthew 16:18

Hades is the same as *Sheol*. In the Hebrew, hell is called *"Sheol"* and in the Greek language it is referred to as *"Hades"*.

Hades is a place of departed souls. *Hades* means "the unseen". *Hades* is the unseen underworld.

Sheol is the place of the dead. *Sheol* is a place of darkness, silence and dust, to which the spirit descends at death. Sheol is likened to a vast family burial site whose entrance is guarded by huge iron gates and bolts. *Sheol* is also likened to a prison in which the dead are held captive by strong cords. The dead in *Sheol* are cut off from the living and from their relationship to God.

1. ***Hades* is an unseen world into which entire cities can disappear.**

   And thou, Capernaum, which art exalted unto heaven, shalt be brought down to hell: for if the mighty works, which have been done in thee, had been done in Sodom, it would have remained until this day.

   Matthew 11:23

2. ***Hades* is the place where the dead are resident.** Hades is also the place where much evil resides. Out of this place proceeds all the wars against the church.

   And I say also unto thee, That thou art Peter, and upon this rock I will build my church; and the gates of hell shall not prevail against it.

   Matthew 16:18

3. ***Hades* is the destination of the rich men who forget God and do not listen to the prophet of God.**

   And in hell he lift up his eyes, being in torments, and seeth Abraham afar off, and Lazarus in his bosom.

   Luke 16:23

4. ***Hades* is the final destination of all living souls.** Jesus was not left there. These scriptures prove that *Sheol* and *Hades* are one and the same thing.

Because thou wilt not leave my soul in HELL (*HADES*), neither wilt thou suffer thine Holy One to see corruption. Thou hast made known to me the ways of life; thou shalt make me full of joy with thy countenance. Men and brethren, let me freely speak unto you of the patriarch David, that he is both dead and buried, and his sepulchre is with us unto this day. Therefore being a prophet, and knowing that God had sworn with an oath to him, that of the fruit of his loins, according to the flesh, he would raise up Christ to sit on his throne; He seeing this before spake of the resurrection of Christ, that his soul was not left in hell, neither his flesh did see corruption.

Acts 2:27-31

Therefore my heart is glad, and my glory rejoiceth: my flesh also shall rest in hope. For thou wilt not leave my soul in HELL (*SHEOL*); neither wilt thou suffer thine Holy One to see corruption.

Psalm 16:9-10

5. ***Hades* is the destination of the dead; the good and the bad.** *Hades* contains all the other compartments of the underworld. It is also called the grave.

O death, where is thy sting? O GRAVE, (*HADES*) where is thy victory?

1 Corinthians 15:55

6. ***Hades* is the general place for all souls who die.** Eventual transfers will take place from Hades to final compartments in the end.

And the sea gave up the dead which were in it; and death and hell delivered up the dead which were in them: and

64

they were judged every man according to their works. And death and hell were cast into the lake of fire. This is the second death.

Revelation 20:13-14

7. *Hades* remains under the ultimate control of Jesus.

I am he that liveth, and was dead; and, behold, I am alive for evermore, Amen; and have the keys of hell and of death.

Revelation 1:18

8. Representatives of hell come marching on earth to take masses of people away.

And I looked, and behold a pale horse: and his name that sat on him was Death, and Hell followed with him. And power was given unto them over the fourth part of the earth, to kill with sword, and with hunger, and with death, and with the beasts of the earth.

Revelation 6:8

CHAPTER 20

Paradise

And Jesus said unto him, Verily I say unto thee, To day shalt thou be with me IN PARADISE.

Luke 23:43

Paradise is a park, a preserve, an enclosed garden. Paradise is a place of future happiness; but there is also the paradise of Hades.

1. **Paradise is the place where Jesus went to when He descended into hell – "the paradise of Hades".**

And Jesus said unto him, Verily I say unto thee, To day shalt thou be with me in paradise.

Luke 23:43

2. **Paradise was the place where Paul was caught up into and saw visions.**

And I knew such a man, (whether in the body, or out of the body, I cannot tell: God knoweth;) How that HE WAS CAUGHT UP INTO PARADISE, and heard unspeakable words, which it is not lawful for a man to utter.

2 Corinthians 12:3-4

3. **Paradise is a place, a park, a preserve which can be either up or down.** "There is the paradise of God". The paradise of God is the garden and preserve of God. The paradise of Hades is probably where Jesus descended into when He died on the cross.

He that hath an ear, let him hear what the Spirit saith unto the churches; To him that overcometh will I give to eat of the tree of life, which is in the midst of THE PARADISE OF GOD.

Revelation 2:7

CHAPTER 21

The Bottomless Pit:
The Abyss, Abussos

And cast him into the BOTTOMLESS PIT, and shut him up, and set a seal upon him, that he should deceive the nations no more,...

Revelation 20:3

1. The bottomless pit is a place where demons are held and tortured.

And the fifth angel sounded, and I saw a star fall from heaven unto the earth: and to him was given THE KEY OF THE BOTTOMLESS PIT. And he opened the bottomless pit; and there arose a smoke out of the pit, as the smoke of a great furnace; and the sun and the air were darkened by reason of the smoke of the pit. And THERE CAME OUT OF THE SMOKE LOCUSTS UPON THE EARTH: and unto them was given power, as the scorpions of the earth have power. And it was commanded them that they should not hurt the grass of the earth, neither any green thing, neither any tree; but only those men which have not the seal of God in their foreheads. And to them it was given that they should not kill them, but that they should be tormented five months: and their torment was as the torment of a scorpion, when he striketh a man.

Revelation 9:1-5

There is so much fire in the pit that the smoke from the bottomless pit can darken the sun. Inside this bottomless pit are found evil creatures. These demonic creatures look like locusts and have the power of scorpions to hurt and to torment people.

2. The bottomless pit is a place where Satan will be held for a thousand years.

And I saw an angel come down from heaven, having the key of the bottomless pit and a great chain in his hand. And he laid hold on the dragon, that old serpent, which is the Devil, and Satan, and bound him a thousand years, And cast him into THE BOTTOMLESS PIT, and shut him up, and set a seal upon him, that he should deceive the nations no more, till the thousand years should be fulfilled: and after that he must be loosed a little season.

Revelation 20:1-3

Satan will be in the midst of these scorpion-like demons. Satan will be in a mighty furnace and will burn in everlasting fire for a thousand years in this place.

3. The bottomless pit is where "the beast" will ascend out of.

The beast that thou sawest was, and is not; and shall ascend out of THE BOTTOMLESS PIT, and go into perdition: and they that dwell on the earth shall wonder, whose names were not written in the book of life from the foundation of the world, when they behold the beast that was, and is not, and yet is.

Revelation 17:8

The bottomless pit is the source of the antichrist demon. As you read this book, the antichrist demon has been held in check in the bottomless pit. The bottomless pit is a temporary prison of sorts.

4. The devils in the mad man were really scared of going to the bottomless pit before time.

And Jesus asked him, saying, what is thy name? And he said, Legion: because many devils were entered into him. And they besought him that he would not command them to go out into THE DEEP. And there was there an herd of many swine feeding on the mountain: and they besought him that he would suffer them to enter into them. And he suffered them.

Luke 8:30-32

Demons prefer to be on earth than to be in the bottomless pit. I think that demons have a much better and easier life on earth than they do in the bottomless pit.

5. Jesus went to the deep for us.

Or, who shall descend into THE DEEP? (that is, to bring up Christ again from the dead.)

Romans 10:7

Jesus descended into the bottomless pit for us. Once Jesus was in the bottomless pit, He disarmed the enemy and took the keys to death and hell.

CHAPTER 22

Tartarus

For if God didn't spare the angels who sinned but threw them down into TARTARUS and delivered them to be kept in chains of darkness until judgment;
2 Peter 2:4 (HCSB)

1. ***Tartarus* is the place where those angels who sinned among the angels were put.**

> For if God spared not the angels that sinned, but cast them down to hell (*TARTARUS*), and delivered them into chains of darkness, to be reserved unto judgment; And spared not the old world, but saved Noah the eighth person, a preacher of righteousness, bringing in the flood upon the world of the ungodly;

> 2 Peter 2:4-5

There was a team of angels that invaded the earth and had sex with humans. This was an abomination and God condemned those angels to a special place called *Tartarus*. *Tartarus* is a place of darkness and chains.

2. ***Tartarus* is dark and full of chains.**

> And the angels which kept not their first estate, but left their own habitation, HE HATH RESERVED IN EVERLASTING CHAINS UNDER DARKNESS unto the judgment of the great day.

> Jude 1:6

The scripture is quite clear that the angels who could not stay in the appropriate place were condemned to this special prison called *Tartarus*. In *Tartarus*, these angels are kept in absolute blackness and darkness. They are also bound in chains and are not free to move around as they would like to.

CHAPTER 23

Gehenna

But I say unto you, that whosoever is angry with his brother without a cause shall be in danger of the judgment: and whosoever shall say to his brother, Raca, shall be in danger of the council: but whosoever shall say, Thou fool, shall be in danger of HELL FIRE (*GEHENNA*).

Matthew 5:22

Gehenna is yet another hell. *Gehenna* was originally the valley of Hinnom, south of Jerusalem, where the filth and dead animals of the city were cast out and burned. This became a symbol of the wicked and of their future destruction in hell.

Gehenna is depicted as a scene of rotting dead animals, an extensive rubbish dump with scattered random fires.

1. *Gehenna* is a place of punishment for those who have sinned in their speech.

But I say unto you, that whosoever is angry with his brother without a cause shall be in danger of the judgment: and whosoever shall say to his brother, Raca, shall be in danger of the council: but whosoever shall say, Thou fool, shall be in danger of hell fire.

Matthew 5:22

2. *Gehenna* is a place to be avoided at all costs.

And if thy right eye offend thee, pluck it out, and cast it from thee: for it is profitable for thee that one of thy members should perish, and not that thy whole body should be cast into hell. And if thy right hand offend thee, cut it off, and cast it from thee: for it is profitable for thee that one of thy members should perish, and not that thy whole body should be cast into hell.

Matthew 5:29-30

3. *Gehenna* is a place where both the soul and body are cast into. You recognize dead people because they have bodies.

And fear not them which kill the body, but are not able to kill the soul: but rather fear him which is able to destroy both soul and body in hell.

Matthew 10:28

4. *Gehenna* **is a place to be avoided at all costs**

And if thine eye offend thee, pluck it out, and cast it from thee: it is better for thee to enter into life with one eye, rather than having two eyes to be cast into hell fire.

Matthew 18:9

5. *Gehenna* **is a place that will receive all those serpentine demons.** People who behave like vipers will also end up in *Gehenna*. *Gehenna* is reserved for vipers.

Ye serpents, ye generation of vipers, how can ye escape the damnation of hell?

Matthew 23:33

CHAPTER 24

The Lake of Fire

And if anyone's name was not found written in the book of life, he was thrown into the LAKE OF FIRE.

Revelation 20:15

The lake of fire is the final destination of the wicked, and evil people under the earth and in Hades.

And the devil that deceived them was cast into the lake of fire and brimstone, where the beast and the false prophet are, and shall be tormented day and night for ever and ever. And I saw a great white throne, and him that sat on it, from whose face the earth and the heaven fled away; and there was found no place for them. And I saw the dead, small and great, stand before God; and the books were opened: and another book was opened, which is the book of life: and the dead were judged out of those things which were written in the books, according to their works. And the sea gave up the dead which were in it; and death and hell delivered up the dead which were in them: and they were judged every man according to their works. AND DEATH AND HELL (*HADES*) WERE CAST INTO THE LAKE OF FIRE. This is the second death. And whosoever was not found written in the book of life was cast into the lake of fire.

Revelation 20:10-15

The lake of fire is the final destination of wicked people on earth. It is also the final destination for the devil. The lake of fire is a vast burning sea. Being able to swim will not help you much in the lake of fire. *Hades* and *Sheol* will be transferred into this lake of fire.